★

WHEN ALL THE WORLD'S ASLEEP

A Children's Book of Poems and Prayers

★

*Compiled by
Liz Attenborough*

ELEMENT
CHILDREN'S BOOKS

SHAFTESBURY, DORSET,
BOSTON, MASSACHUSETTS,
MELBOURNE, VICTORIA

For Helen and Nicholas

© Element Children's Books 1998
Introduction and compilation © Liz Attenborough 1998
First published in Great Britain in 1998 as Poems, Prayers and Meditations by Element Children's Books,
Shaftesbury, Dorset SP7 8BP

Published in the USA in 1998 by Element Books Inc.
160 North Washington Street, Boston MA 02114

Published in Australia in 1998 by Element Books Limited and distributed by Penguin Books Australia Ltd,
487 Maroondah Highway, Ringwood, Victoria 3134

This edition published in 1999

Cover illustrations © 1998 Stephen Lambert
Inside illustrations © 1998 Bee Willey, Thomas Taylor, Stephen Lambert, Alan Drummond, Jill Newton,
Colin Williams, Valeria Petrone, Maryclare Foa, Peter Bailey, Rosemary Woods

The moral rights of the compiler and illustrators have been asserted.

British Library Cataloguing in Publication data available.
Library of Congress Cataloging in Publication data available.
ISBN 1 9026 1873 4

Cover and text design by Mandy Sherliker
Printed in China

CONTENTS

INTRODUCTION

Childhood is a time of great discovery and joy, but also a time of some confusion
and anxiety. This anthology of poems, prayers and meditations recognizes the
variety of emotions children will encounter, and seeks to reflect some of the
feelings and thoughts likely to be bubbling just under the
surface of their day-to-day lives.

Any collections such as this can only be a personal choice, and I have tried to
select pieces that have something to say to make the reader stop for a while and
reflect. Poetry can give fresh meaning to ordinary, everyday experiences of life,
and its music can draw us in so that we share the poet's thoughts and relate them
to ourselves. For the most part I have chosen pieces with a particular compassion,
but some poems have been chosen just because they made me smile,
and I hope they make you smile too.

Each section of the book ends with a meditation, specially written for this book,
that will allow you to calmly reflect on the emotions stirred by the words of
others. Give yourself a special time to relax and explore your own imagination.

This book presents just a tiny portion of the great wealth of poetry written in the
English language, and there is never a time when there isn't more to discover and
delight in. Any library or bookshop will have a huge selection of books of poetry
to suit every taste. You can make your own anthology of poems and prayers by
including pieces that you like, that make you laugh, that say something special to
you, or that you know you would like to share with someone else. Write them in
a book of your own and soon you will build a very special collection. Look at it in
years to come and your eye and mind will respond to new things – an image, an
idea that has taken on a new meaning for you as you grow and change.
The best will stay with you forever.

Note to Adults on the Meditations

To make the most of the meditations, you and your child should find a quiet place
where you won't be disturbed. Either lying down or sitting up straight, your child
should have his or her eyes closed and take deep, slow breaths – in through the nose, out
through the mouth – trying all the time to relax body and limbs so that they become
calm and centered. As you read the meditation keep your voice soft but audible and
speak slowly, with frequent pauses. When you have finished reading give the child time
to be absorbed in silence before quietly getting up and going back to everyday life.

ALL THE WORDS YOU EVER WILL HEAR

All that we ought to have thought and have not thought,
All that we ought to have said, and have not said,
All that we ought to have done, and have not done,
All that we ought not to have thought, and yet have thought,
All that we ought not to have said, and yet have said,
All that we ought not to have done, and have yet done,
For all these words, and deeds, O God,
We pray for forgiveness,
and repent with penance.

Ascribed to Zoroaster, 1500 SC

I am the Song

I am the song that sings the bird.
I am the leaf that grows the land.
I am the tide that moves the moon.
I am the stream that halts the sand.
I am the cloud that drives the storm.
I am the earth that lights the sun.
I am the fire that strikes the stone.
I am the clay that shapes the hand.
I am the word that speaks the man.

Charles Causley

Twenty-six Letters

Twenty-six cards in half a pack;
Twenty-six weeks in half a year;
Twenty-six letters dressed in black
In all the words you ever will hear.

In "King", "Queen", "Ace", and "Jack",
In "London", "lucky", "lone", and "lack",
"January", "April", "fortify", "fix",
You'll never find more than twenty-six.

Think of the beautiful things you see
On mountain, riverside, meadow and tree.
How many their names are, but how small
The twenty-six letters that spell them all.

James Reeves

When I open my mouth
every word that I say
paints a picture of me
for the others that day.
If I die, all the colours
are shaded with grey
and the light and the life
fade away from the day.
If the words that I say
are the truth then they see
a clear likeness of God
in the picture of me.

Traditional

I asked the little boy who cannot see

I asked the little boy who cannot see,
"And what is colour like?"
"Why, green," said he,
"Is like the rustle when the wind blows through
The forest; running water, that is blue;
And red is like a trumpet sound; and pink
Is like the smell of roses; and I think
That purple must be like a thunderstorm;
And yellow is like something soft and warm;
And white is a pleasant stillness when you lie
And dream."

Anonymous

The Word Party

Loving words clutch crimson roses,
Rude words sniff and pick their noses,
Sly words come dressed up as foxes,
Short words stand on cardboard boxes,
Common words tell jokes and gabble,
Complicated words play Scrabble,
Swear words stamp around and shout,
Hard words stare each other out,
Foreign words look lost and shrug,
Careless words trip on the rug,
Long words slouch with stooping shoulders,
Code words carry secret folders,
Silly words flick rubber bands,
Hyphenated words hold hands,
Strong words show off, bending metal,
Sweet words call each other "petal,"
Small words yawn and suck their thumbs
Till at last the morning comes,
Kind words give out farewell posies . . .

Snap! The dictionary closes.

Richard Edwards

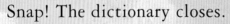

Reading

A story is a special thing.
 The ones that I have read,
They do not stay inside the book,
 They stay inside my head.

Marchette Chute

A Poem in My Pocket

I've a poem in my pocket,
And another in my head;
They come and go sometimes,
When I'm lying in my bed.

I waken in the morning
With a thought as new as day;
By the time I've had my cornflakes,
It's faded quite away.

John Cunliffe

11

An Attempt At Unrhymed Verse

People tell you all the time,
Poems do not have to rhyme.
It's often better if they don't
And I'm determined this one won't.
                              Oh dear.

Never mind, I'll start again.
Busy, busy with my pen...cil.
I can do it if I try –
Easy, peasy, pudding and gherkins.

Writing verse is so much fun,
Cheering as the summer weather,
Makes you feel alert and bright,
'Specially when you get it more or less the
                              way you want it.

Wendy Cope

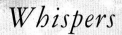

Whispers

Whispers
    tickle through your ear
    telling things you like to hear

Whispers
    are as soft as skin
    letting little words curl in.

Whispers
    come so they can blow
    secrets others never know.

Myra Cohn Livingston

W

The King sent for his Wise Men all
    To find a rhyme for W;
When they had thought a good long time
But could not think of a single rhyme,
    "I'm sorry," said he, "to trouble you."

James Reeves

I AM THE SONG

Find a quiet space and sit or lie down with your back straight and close your eyes. Breathe slowly and deeply and begin to feel calm and quiet. Imagine you are walking along the seashore early one morning, looking at how the tracks of birds begin in the sand, go on and then end suddenly. Across the blue water soft words of music come in, riding on the white waves rolling up the beach. As you listen to the sound you look further up the shore where a tree standing alone spreads its shade over a patch of rocks. Just as you sit under the tree, a tiny new leaf unfolds and the sun and the wind breathe on it gently to welcome it to its new life.

The song of the birds and the new green leaf greet you to their world, and you sit and watch the morning tide come in as the last slice of the moon calls goodbye and the sun climbs higher in the sky.

The flat stones by your feet want to be friends too and you wonder what it would be like to listen to a stone talk. Over by the river that flows to the sea, the song of the gushing water is almost drowned as hundreds of birds gather to meet you. Then there is a rushing, swishing sound as a cloud of silver wings rolls across the sky. You hear the song becoming a gentle roar and a storm grows as the sun and the earth touch and greet each other. Everywhere all the creatures are singing and suddenly you can understand. You feel that maybe everything is part of everything else and it all belongs together, and it is all inside your heart. Keep that warm feeling in your heart and rest quietly with it.
Whenever you are ready, open your eyes.

Florence Hamilton

SOMETHING

ABOUT

ME

I Thank you Lord

I thank you Lord, for knowing me
      better than I know myself,
And for letting me know myself
      better than others know me.
Make me, I ask you then,
      better than others know me.
Make me, I ask you then,
      better than they suppose,
And forgive me for what they do not know.

A Muslim prayer

Something About Me

There's something about me
      That I'm knowing.
There's something about me
      That isn't showing.

    I'm growing!

Anonymous

16

Jump or Jiggle

Frogs jump
Caterpillars hump

Worms wiggle
Bugs jiggle

Rabbits hop
Horses clop

Snakes slide
Sea-gulls glide

Mice creep
Deer leap

Puppies bounce
Kittens pounce

Lions stalk –
But –
I walk!

Evelyn Beyer

My Puppy

It's funny
my puppy
knows just how I feel.

When I'm happy
he's yappy
and squirms like an eel.

When I'm grumpy
he's slumpy
and stays at my heel.

It's funny
my puppy
knows such a great deal.

Aileen Fisher

The Secret Place

There's a place I go, inside myself,
    Where nobody else can be,
And none of my friends can tell it's there –
    Nobody knows but me.

It's hard to explain the way it feels,
    Or even where I go.
It isn't a place in time or space,
    But once I'm there, *I know.*

It's tiny, it's shiny, it can't be seen,
    But it's big as the sky at night ...
I try to explain and it hurts my brain,
    But once I'm there, it's *right.*

There's a place I know inside myself,
    And it's neither big nor small,
And whenever I go, it feels as though
    I never left at all.

Dennis Lee

Prayer

O Divine Master, grant that
I may not so much seek
to be consoled as to console;
to be understood as to understand;
to be loved, as to love;
for it is in giving that we receive,
it is in pardoning that we
are pardoned, and it is in dying
that we are born to eternal life.

St. Francis of Assisi

18

Friends

I fear it's very wrong of me
And yet I must admit
When someone offers friendship
I want the *whole* of it.
I don't want everybody else
To share my friends with me.
At least, I want *one* special one,
Who, indisputably
      Likes me much more than all the rest,
Who's always on my side.
Who never cares what others say,
Who lets me come and hide
Within his shadow, in his house –
It doesn't matter where –
Who let's me simply be myself,
Who's always, *always* there.

Elizabeth Jennings

A Blessing

God bless all those that I love;
God bless all those that love me;
God bless all those that love those that I love,
All those that love those that love me.

Anonymous

The Secret Brother

Jack lived in the green-house
When I was six,
With glass and with tomato plants,
Not with slates and bricks.

I didn't have a brother,
Jack became mine.
Nobody could see him,
He never gave a sign.

Just beyond the rockery,
By the apple-tree,
Jack and his old mother lived,
Only for me.

With a tin telephone
Held beneath the sheet,
I would talk to Jack each night.
We would never meet.

Once my sister caught me,
Said, "He isn't there.
Down among the flower-pots
Cramm the gardener

Is the only person."
I said nothing, but
Let her go on talking.
Yet I moved Jack out.

He and his old mother
Did a midnight flit.
No one knew his number:
I had altered it.

Only I could see
The sagging washing-line
And my brother making
Our own secret sign.

Elizabeth Jennings

Dear Mum,

while you were out
a cup went and broke itself,
a crack appeared in the blue vase
your great-great grandad
brought back from Mr. Ming in China.
Somehow, without me even turning on the tap,
the sink mysteriously overflowed.
A strange jam-stain,
about the size of a boy's hand,
appeared on the kitchen wall.
I don't think we will ever discover
exactly how the cat
managed to turn on the washing-machine
(specially from the inside),
or how Sis's pet rabbit went and mistook
the waste-disposal unit for a burrow.
I can tell you I was scared when,
as if by magic,
a series of muddy footprints
appeared on the new white carpet.
I was being good
(honest)
but I think the house is haunted so
knowing you're going to have a fit
I've gone over to Gran's for a bit.

Brian Patten

The House I Go to in My Dream

The house I go to in my dream
stands beside a little stream
full of dab and minnow and
trout I try to catch by hand
but every single fish is
more elusive than my wishes.

For every time I wish, you see,
I wish that someone else was me.
I stand and wish and call up spells
to turn me into something else
but no matter how I try
I finish up remaining I,
however hard I wish to be
someone else, I am still me.

And so I think that I and you
and every other person, too,
must really be a sort of fish
not to be caught just with a wish.

George Barker

If I were a butterfly,
I'd thank you, Lord, for giving me wings,
and if I were a robin in a tree,
I'd thank you, Lord, that I could sing,
and if I were a fish in the sea,
I'd wiggle my tail and I'd giggle with glee,
but I just thank you, Father, for making me 'me'.

Brian Howard

I Meant to Do My Work Today

I meant to do my work today –
But a brown bird sang in the apple tree,
And a butterfly flitted across the field,
And the leaves were calling me.

And the wind went sighing over the land,
Tossing the grasses to and fro,
And a rainbow held out its shining hand –
So what could I do but laugh and go?

Richard le Gallienne

The Knight's Prayer

God be in my head,
    And in my understanding;

God be in mine eyes,
    And in my looking;

God be in my mouth,
    And in my speaking;

God be in my heart,
    And in my thinking;

God be at my end,
    And at my departing.

Anonymous

A SECRET PLACE TO BE

Go to a quiet place and sit or lie down with your back straight. Close the eyes. Breathe slowly and deeply and begin to feel calm and centered. You are in charge and nothing can happen that you don't want to happen.

Imagine you are walking outside on a warm spring day. Feel the path under your feet as you walk and the soft leaves brushing you as you go by. Follow the path until you come to a gate almost hidden in the bushes. You reach out and push it open. Somehow you know that you are in a place where no one has ever been before. It is your place. You find yourself in a beautiful garden which is just the way you would like a garden to be. Take a few minutes to let your mind's eye wander over the grass, trees, bushes and flowers. It is yours – make it as you want it to be.

Just then you notice a building at the far side of the garden and you start to walk towards it. This is your special house – it could be a little hut or a cottage, a house or a castle. As you walk towards it, notice the details of your house – the roof, windows, what are the walls made of? Walk up to the front door and feel the handle under your touch. Turn the handle and notice any sounds as you push the door open and walk inside.

You feel as if you are coming home – a feeling of intense happiness and joy fills your heart. As you look around you know that this secret place is yours alone and no-one else has ever been here – or ever will unless you ask them. Take a bit of time to wander through the rooms. What are they like? Are they full or empty? Put your favourite treasures in the house.

Go into one particular room where there is a deep, comfortable armchair. Sit down and feel the cushions supporting you. Put your attention in your heart and notice the breath coming in and going out. You feel deeply at peace. You know that everything is just fine, you can cope with anything the world may send you.

Gently retrace your steps out through the door, back down the garden, along the path and open your eyes and look around you. You feel light and carefree and ready for anything. You know you can return to the secret place any time you want. It is your special place.

Caroline Mann

A
JOYFUL
DAY

Daybreak

The moon shines bright,
The stars give light
Before the break of day;
God bless you all
Both great and small
And send you a joyful day.

Traditional

Singing-Time

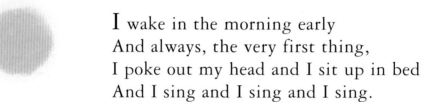

I wake in the morning early
And always, the very first thing,
I poke out my head and I sit up in bed
And I sing and I sing and I sing.

Rose Fyleman

Good-Morning

Good-morning now.
Wake, body,
Wake, mind!
Work, play,
Seek, find,
Eat breakfast,
Dinner too,
Wash, brush,
Sing, dance, and do!
Good-morning now.

Eleanor Farjeon

Morning

Will there really be a morning?
    Is there such a thing as day?
Could I see it from the mountains
    If I were as tall as they?
Has it feet like water lilies?
    Has it feathers like a bird?
Is it brought from famous countries
    Of which I've never heard?
Oh, some scholar! Oh, some sailor!
    Oh, some wise man from the skies!
Please to tell a little pilgrim
    Where the place called morning lies!

Emily Dickinson

Waking Up

Oh! I have just had such a lovely dream!
And then I woke,
And all the dream went out like kettle-steam,
Or chimney-smoke.

My dream was all about – how funny, though!
I've only just
Dreamed it, and now it has begun to blow
Away like dust.

In it I went – no! in my dream I had –
No, that's not it!
I can't remember, oh, it is *too* bad,
My dream a bit.

But I saw something beautiful, I'm sure –
Then someone spoke,
And then I didn't see it anymore,
Because I woke.

Eleanor Farjeon

I've got a Cold

I've got a cold
And it's not funny

My throat is numb
My nose is runny

My ears are burning
My fingers are itching

My teeth are wobbly
My eyebrows are twitching

My kneecaps have slipped
My bottom's like jelly

The button's come off
My silly old belly

My chin has doubled
My toes are twisted

My ankles have swollen
My elbows are blistered

My back is all spotty
My hair's turning white

I sneeze through the day
And cough through the night

I've got a cold
And I'm going insane

(Apart from all that
I'm right as rain.)

Roger McGough

Goodness

Goodness, love, grace and gentleness,
    Courtesy, friendship and modesty,
Honesty, penance and chastity, charity,
respect, reverence and truthfulness,
Purity and self-control, wisdom and worship –
All these together are perfect virtue,
    and are the word of the loving Lord.

A Hindu prayer

Questions

Do trains get tired of running
And woodworms tired of holes
Do tunnels tire of darkness
And stones of being so old?

Do shadows tire of sunshine
And puddles tire of rain?
And footballs tire of kicking
Does Peter tire of Jane?

Does water tire of spilling
And fires of being too hot
And smells get tired of smelling
And chickenpox – of spots?

I do not know the answers
I'll ask them all one day . . .
But I get tired of reading
And I've done enough today.

Peter Dixon

30

On the Move

Can't stop; hurry, scurrying
Underneath the day,
Got to hide myself before
The sun gives me away,
Got to find some shelter
Where the hungry hawk can't prey,
Can't stop; hurry, scurrying
Underneath the day.

Can't stop; hurry, scurrying
Underneath the night,
Got to hide myself before
The moon's too big and bright,
Got to find some shelter
Where the beastly fox can't bite,
Can't stop; hurry, scurrying
Underneath the night.

Can't stop; hurry, scurrying,
Always moving hole,
How long can I last before
This rushing takes its toll?
Wonder if in heaven
There'll be time to lounge and stroll;
One thing's sure: whoever made this world
Was not a vole.

Richard Edwards

Good Night, Good Night

The dark is dreaming.
    Day is done.
Good night, good night
    To everyone.

Good night to the birds,
    And the fish in the sea,
Good night to the bears
    And goodnight to me.

Dennis Lee

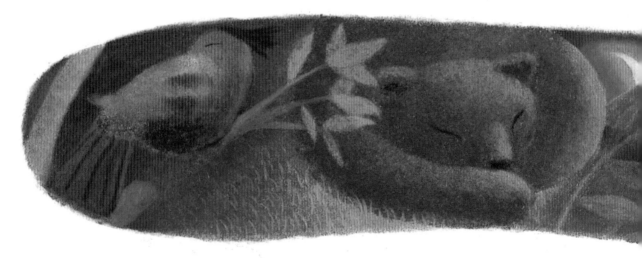

A Child's Prayer

Father, we thank Thee for the night
And for the pleasant morning light,
For rest and food and loving care,
And all that makes the world so fair.
Help us to do the things we should.
To be to others kind and good,
In all we do, in all we say,
To grow more loving every day.

Anonymous

32

At Night

When night is dark
my cat is wise
to light the lanterns
in his eyes

Aileen Fisher

Today and Tomorrow

Happy the man, and happy he alone,
  He who can call today his own;
He who, secure within, can say,
  Tomorrow, do thy worst, for I have lived today.

John Dryden

A GIFT

Find a comfortable position, with your spine straight, and place one hand
on your tummy and one on your heart. Now relax your body and all your
limbs and feel your tummy move underneath your hand as you breathe.
Feel your heart underneath your other hand . . . breathe easily,
relax and close your eyes.

Imagine a beautiful path in nature. It can be anywhere you want it to be
. . . now walk down that path until you come to a big tree – this is your
trouble tree, the tree where you hang up all your troubles. Stop by this
tree and hang up any worries, problems or difficulties you have . . . this
tree can hold anything that doesn't feel good to you, so hang it all up . . .
Now, continue on down your path until you come to a bridge. This is a
magic bridge that only you can cross, for it takes you to your own special
place. You cross the bridge and step into the most beautiful place you
have ever seen! Slowly you wander through it, feeling the ground beneath
your feet, enjoying the lovely colors, scents and sounds around you. Soon
you come to a clearing with a large rock in the center. As you move closer,
you notice a beautiful light beam shining through the trees onto the rock.
Is it a sunbeam or a moonbeam? You move closer and see a small package
on top of the rock. It is a gift for you! You step into the light beam and
feel a warm glow surrounding you and filling you up. Carefully you reach
out to take the gift. Feel the texture of the wrapping as you gently lift it.
Is it heavy or light? You sit down on the rock, place your gift in your lap
and carefully remove the wrapping. Now . . . what wonderful gift do you
see? It is very special and just for you. It helps you remember many other
things that make you happy . . . feel yourself filling up with joy as
you enjoy your gift and your happy thoughts.

As you prepare to leave your special place, hold that joyful feeling in
your heart and take it with you. Now place your gift in a safe place where
it will remain until you return. Thank your special place . . . and bring
the good feeling back into your heart and into this room.
Can you feel the feeling in your heart, beneath your hand?
Whenever you're ready, you can open your eyes.

Jennifer Day

I HATE
AND
I LOVE

I Hate and I Love

I hate and I love.
And if you ask me how,
I do not know: I only feel it,
and I'm torn in two.

Catullus

Poem

I loved my friend
He went away from me
There's nothing more to say.
The poem ends,
Soft as it began –
I loved my friend.

Langston Hughes

Sometimes

Sometimes I simply have to cry,
I don't know why,
I don't know why.
There's really nothing very wrong,
I probably should sing a song
or run around and make some noise
or sit and tinker with my toys
or pop a couple of balloons
or play a game or watch cartoons,
but I'm feeling sad,
though I don't know why,
and all I want to do is cry.

Jack Prelutsky

Betty At The Party

"When I was at the party,"
      Said Betty, aged just four,
"A little girl fell off her chair
      Right down upon the floor;
And all the other little girls
      Began to laugh, but me –
I didn't laugh a single bit,"
      Said Betty seriously.

"Why not?" her mother asked her,
      Full of delight to find
That Betty – bless her little heart! –
      Had been so sweetly kind.
"Why didn't you laugh, my darling?
      Or don't you like to tell?"
"I didn't laugh," said Betty,
      " 'Cause me it was that fell."

Anonymous

Look Out!

The witches mumble horrid chants,
You're scolded by five thousand aunts,
 A Martian pulls a fearsome face
 And hurls you into Outer Space,
You're tied in front of whistling trains,
A tomahawk has sliced your brains,
 The tigers snarl, the giants roar,
 You're sat on by a dinosaur.
In vain you're shouting "Help" and "Stop,"
The walls are spinning like a top,
 The earth is melting in the sun
 And all the horror's just begun.
And, oh, the screams, the thumping hearts
That awful night before school starts.

Max Fatchen

All of Us

All of us are afraid
More often than we tell.

There are times we cling like mussels to the sea-wall,
And pray that the pounding waves
Won't smash our shell.

Times we hear nothing but the sound
Of our loneliness, like a cracked bell
From fields far away where the trees are in icy shade.

O many a time in the night-time and in the day,
More often than we say,
We are afraid.

If people say they are never frightened,
I don't believe them.
If people say they are frightened,
I want to retrieve them

From that dark shivering haunt
Where they don't want to be,
Nor I.

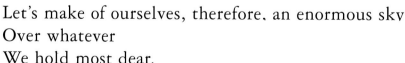

Let's make of ourselves, therefore, an enormous sky
Over whatever
We hold most dear.

And we'll comfort each other,
Comfort each other's
Fear.

Kit Wright

Bubble Poem

When my head is full of troubles
And my heart is full of care
I blow bubbles
Lovely bubbles
Floating floating in the air

When the world is harsh and angry
And nobody seems to care
I blow bubbles
Rainbow bubbles
Floating floating everywhere

Bubbles always make us happy
When we find it hard to cope
For inside each perfect circle
Lies a little ray of hope

When the night is dark and lonely
And the shadows make you cry
Just blow bubbles
Rainbow bubbles
Floating floating in the sky

Ann Ziety

The Giggles

A giggler gets the giggles
    At every little thing –
A puppy dog that sneezes,
    A cow that tries to sing.

She giggles at an elephant,
    She giggles at a toad.
She giggles if a baby duck
    Waddles down a road.

She giggles if the teacher asks
    If two and two are four.
At lunch she giggles if she spills
    Potatoes on the floor.

When mother sat on Daddy's hat
    She giggled till she cried.
I think she ate a feather that
    Is tickling her inside!

Martin Gardner

Bursting

We've laughed until my cheeks are tight.
We've laughed until my stomach's sore.
If only we could stop we might
Remember what we're laughing for.

Dorothy Aldis

Laughing Time

It was laughing time, and the tall Giraffe
Lifted his head, and began to laugh:

Ha! Ha! Ha! Ha!

And the Chimpanzee on the ginkgo tree
Swung merrily down with a *Tee Hee Hee* :

"It's certainly not against the law!"
Croaked Justice Crow with a load guffaw:

Haw! Haw! Haw! Haw!

The dancing Bear who could never say "No"
Waltzed up and down on the tip of his toe:

Ho! Ho! Ho! Ho!

The Donkey daintily took his paw,
And around they went: Hee-Haw! Hee-Haw!

Hee-Haw! Hee-Haw!

The Moon had to smile as it started to climb;
All over the world it was laughing time!

Ho! Ho! Ho! Ho! Hee-Haw! Hee-Haw!
Hee! Hee! Hee! Hee! Ha! Ha! Ha! Ha!

William Jay Smith

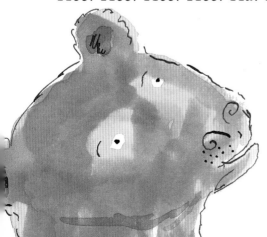

43

Celebration

is daring
to be
who we are
it's like dancing
on table tops
while the world spins
and the fear stops
and the waves crash
and the stars glow
and the heart beats
and inside your head
you hear this song
rising
up
like laughter
rising
up
like a firework
soaring and weightless
to fill the whole sky
with joy

Ann Ziety

Remember

Remember me when I am gone away,
    Gone far away into the silent land;
    When you can no more hold me by the hand,
Nor I half turn to go yet turning stay.
Remember me when no more day by day
    You tell me of our future that you planned:
    Only remember me; you understand
It will be late to counsel then or pray.
Yet if you should forget me for a while
    And afterwards remember, do not grieve:
    For if the darkness and corruption leave
    A vestige of the thoughts that once I had,
Better by far you should forget and smile
    Than that you should remember and be sad.

Christina Rossetti

Night

The night has a thousand eyes,
    And the day but one;
Yet the light of the bright world dies
    With the dying sun.

The mind has a thousand eyes,
    And the heart but one;
Yet the light of a whole life dies,
    When love is done.

Francis William Bourdillon

THE FEELING BUILDING

Relax in a nice, comfortable position, sitting or lying down on your back. With one hand on your tummy and one on your heart, breathe naturally and close your eyes. Now picture, in your imagination, a beautiful scene in nature – whatever you like, a beach, rolling hills, a forest, a garden, a meadow, or any other scene in nature. It can be anywhere you want, exactly the way you want it to be, and it is perfectly safe. Walk through your scene until you come upon a pathway and begin to walk along it. In the distance you see a beautiful building. Slowly you approach the building, admiring its beauty and knowing that it too, is perfectly safe. You step up to the front door and see a sign. It says, "The Feeling Building." You enter the building. There are many rooms in this building and on each door is a sign with a feeling written on it. One says "Care," another "Hurt," one says "Jealousy," the next one "Joy." There is "Frustration," "Anger," "Hate," and "Love," and all the other feelings you know of – each one with its own door. You choose one of the doors with a feeling you have that you'd like to change. You open the door and step inside. There before you is a bare room and in this room you see – yourself! You watch yourself having the feeling you chose. See how your face looks, how your body feels, and what you are doing. You decide to change the scene. You see yourself instead doing something you love to do, being in your favorite place or cuddling your favorite animal. See how happy you are! How does your face look now? How does your body feel? . . . You know now that whenever you feel yourself having a feeling that you don't like or that you want to change, you can change! Leave the room now, with yourself happy inside. As you close the door, you notice that the sign now says "Love."

Go back into your beautiful nature scene. Anything that you enjoy and love can be there. Have a wonderful time and enjoy the feeling of being there! . . . Now bring your attention back to your breathing and see if you can feel the wonderful feeling in your heart. Feel your heart beating and whenever you're ready, open your eyes.

Jennifer Day

ALL
THE
PEOPLE
THAT I
LOVE

Song in Space

When man first flew beyond the sky
He looked back into the world's blue eye.
Man said: What makes your eye so blue?
Earth said: The tears in the oceans do.
Why are the seas so full of tears?
Because I've wept so many thousand years.
Why do you weep as you dance through space?
Because I am the Mother of the Human Race.

Adrian Mitchell

Squeezes

We love to squeeze bananas,
We love to squeeze ripe plums,
And when they are feeling sad
We love to squeeze our mums.

Brian Patten

Love Me – I Love You

Love me – I love you,
        Love me, my baby;
Sing it high, sing it low,
        Sing it as may be.

Mother's arms under you;
        Her eyes above you;
Sing it high, sing it low,
        Love me – I love you.

Christina Rossetti

How Many Stars?

When I was a boy
I would ask my dad:
"How many stars are there hanging in the sky?"
          "More than enough, son,
          More than I could say.
          Enough to keep you counting
          Till your dying day."

When I was a boy
I would ask my dad:
"How many fishes are there swimming in the sea?"
          "More than enough, son,
          More than I could say.
          Enough to keep you counting
          Till your dying day."

When I was a boy
I would ask my dad:
"How many creepy-crawlies are there in the world?"
          "More than enough, son,
          More than I could say.
          Enough to keep you counting
          Till your dying day."

It seemed like there wasn't anything my dad didn't know.

Colin McNaughton

Home

Home to laughter, home to rest,
Home to those we love the best,
Home to where there is none to hate,
Where no foes in anguish wait,
Where no jealous envious mind
Seeks with glee a fault to find.
Now the day is done and I
Turn to hear a welcoming cry.
Love is dancing at the door,
I am safe at home once more.

Margaret Fishback Powers

The Very Nicest Place

The fish lives in the brook,
The bird lives in the tree,
But home's the very nicest place
For a little child like me.

Anonymous

Dear Lord, I'd like to pray
for all the people that I love,
but who live far away.
Tonight with them my thoughts I share,
Please keep them in your loving care,
Each night and every day.

Traditional

My Friend

my friend is
like bark
rounding a tree

he warms
like sun
on a winter day

he cools
like water
in the hot noon

his voice
is ready
as a spring bird

he is
my friend
and I
am his

Emily Hearn

51

Brother

I had a little brother
And I brought him to my mother
And I said I want another
Little brother for a change.
But she said don't be a bother
So I took him to my father
And I said this little bother
Of a brother's very strange.

But he said one little brother
Is exactly like another
And every little brother
Misbehaves a bit he said.
So I took the little bother
From my mother and my father
And I put the little bother
Of a brother back to bed.

Mary Ann Hobermann

Some Things Don't Make Any Sense at All

My mum says I'm her sugarplum.
My mum says I'm her lamb.
My mum says I'm completely perfect
Just the way I am.
My mum says I'm a super-special wonderful terrific little guy.
My mum just had another baby.
Why?

Judith Viorst

52

Urgent Note To My Parents

Don't ask me to do what I can't do
Only ask me to do what I can
Don't ask me to be what I can't be
Only ask me to be what I am

Don't one minute say "Be a big girl"
And the next "You're too little for that"
PLEASE don't ask me to be where I can't be
PLEASE be happy with right where I'm at.

Hiawyn Oram

Father, bless me to the dawn
Bless me to the coming morn
Bless all that my eyes will see.
Bless all that will come to me.
Bless my neighbour and my friend.
Bless until our journey's end.
Bless the traveller to our shore.
Bless the stranger at our door.
Bless me to the opening year.
Bless all to me who are dear.
Bless, O Lord, this day of days.
Bless with riches all our ways.

David Adam

When we go over
to my grandads
he falls asleep.

While he's asleep
he snores.

When he wakes up,
he says,
"Did I snore?
did I snore?
did I snore?"

Everybody says, "No,
you didn't snore."

Why do we lie to him?

Michael Rosen

Granny

It so nice to have a Granny
when you've had it from yuh Mammy
and you feeling down and dammy.

It so nice to have a Granny
when she bring you bread and jammy
and says, "Tell it all to Granny."

Grace Nichols

Grandad

Grandad's dead
And I'm sorry about that.

He'd a huge black overcoat.
He felt proud in it.
You could have hidden
A football crowd in it.
Far too big –
It was a lousy fit
But Grandad didn't
Mind a bit.
He wore it all winter
With a squashed black hat.

Now he's dead
And I'm sorry about that.

He'd got twelve stories.
I'd heard every one of them
Hundreds of times
But that was the fun of them:
You knew what was coming
So you could join in.
He'd got big hands
And brown, grooved skin
And when he laughed
It knocked you flat.

Now he's dead
And I'm sorry about that.

Kit Wright

LOVE WEB

Find a comfortable position, with your spine straight, and relax your whole
body. Place one hand on your heart and one on your tummy, and close
your eyes. As you breathe, notice your heart underneath your hand and
think about something that makes you feel really good – like a hug from
someone you love, a special place you love to go, or a cuddle with your
favorite pet. Notice how that makes you feel and see if you can spread
that feeling out through your chest . . . and then through your
whole body, all the way out to your fingers and toes!

Enjoy that wonderful feeling as it fills your body. Let yourself enjoy
it so much that you begin to feel like expanding to hold all that good
feeling! Imagine your body growing, expanding, and reaching out until
you are large enough to embrace every single person that you love, all
at the same time! Feel all that love you have in your heart reaching out
to all the people that you love. Notice how it makes them feel, and how
good it feels to you when the love comes back to you, ten times stronger
than it was when you sent it out. . . Notice how the love you feel
connects you all to each other, like a giant web. Enjoy basking
in this feeling for a moment . . .

Now, allow all the people that you love to carry on with the rest of
their day, feeling so much better for all the love they have received from
you. Quietly thank them all for being in your life. Now bring your
attention back to your heart. Feel yourself returning to your normal
size, holding that good feeling inside you all the time.
Can you feel the feeling anywhere else in your body? . . .
Whenever you're ready, open your eyes.

Jennifer Day

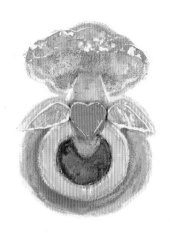

HELP

ALONG

A

BROTHER

. . . I have a dream that one day this nation will rise up and live out the true meaning of its creed: We hold these truths to be self-evident; that all men are created equal.

. . . I have a dream that one day my four little children will one day live in a nation where they will not be judged by the colour of their skin but by the content of their character.

Martin Luther King 1963

Coloured

When I was born, I was black.
When I grew up, I was black.
When I get hot, I am black.
When I get cold, I am black.
When I am sick, I am black.
When I die, I am black.

When you were born, You were pink.
When you grew up, You were white.
When you get hot, You go red.
When you get cold, You go blue.
When you are sick, You go purple.
When you die, You go green.

AND YET YOU HAVE THE CHEEK TO CALL *ME* COLOURED!!!

Anonymous, U5Z, King Edward VI School, Handsworth, Birmingham, UK.

He Who Loses Money

He who loses money,
loses much.

He who loses a friend,
loses more.

But he who loses spirit,
loses all.

Traditional

A Wise Old Owl

A wise old owl sat in an oak,
The more he heard, the less he spoke;
The less he spoke, the more he heard.
Why aren't we all like that wise old bird?

Anonymous

First the seed
and then the grain;
Thank you, God,
for sun and rain.
First the flour
and then the bread;
Thank you, God,
That we are fed.
Thank you, God,
for all your care;
help us all
to share and share.

Traditional

from *Gotta Serve Somebody*

You may be an ambassador to England or France,
You may like to gamble, you might like to dance,
You may be the heavyweight champion of the world,
You may be a socialite with a long string of pearls

But you're gonna have to serve somebody, yes indeed
You're gonna have to serve somebody,
Well, it may be the devil or it may be the Lord
But you're gonna have to serve somebody.

. . .You may be a state trooper, you might be a young Turk,
You may be the head of some big TV network,
You may be rich or poor, you may be blind or lame,
You may be living in another country under another name

But you're gonna serve somebody, yes indeed
You're gonna serve somebody,
Well, it may be the devil or it may be the Lord
But you're gonna have to serve somebody.

Bob Dylan

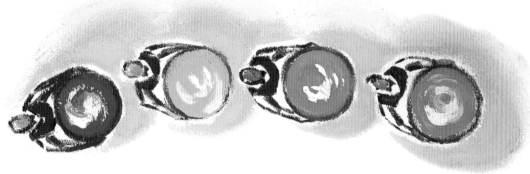

An open foe may prove a curse,
But a pretended friend is worse.

Benjamin Franklin

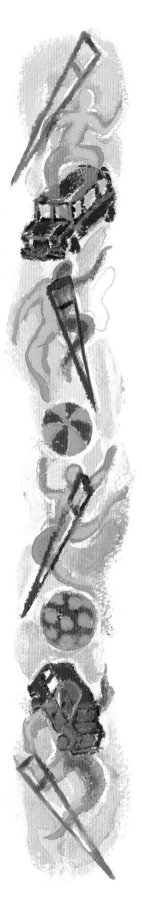

Kieran

Kieran can't walk like the rest of us
He comes to school on the special bus.

He has to use crutches to get about
And he's fast, but he can't keep up when we run
When we race in the wind and laugh and have fun
He can't keep up, he has to shout
"Wait for me everyone, wait for me."
And sometimes we wait, and sometimes we

Run off and hide, and that's when he
Sits in the yard with his sticks on the ground
Sits by himself until he's found
By Sir or Miss, and they sit and talk
And we watch him laugh in a special way
And we'd love to know what he has to say

About the ones who ran away,
The ones who forgot that he can't walk.
And then we remember to ask him to play.
We kick the ball and he hits it back.
He's quick with his sticks, he has the knack
Of whamming the ball right into the goal.

And if he falls over he doesn't fuss
We hoist him back up and we laugh at the soil
On his hands and knees, and give him his sticks.
He pretends to fight us, but he never kicks.

He can't use his legs like the rest of us.
He comes to school on the special bus.

Berlie Doherty

Mother Teresa's Prayer

Make us worthy, Lord,
To serve our fellow-men
Throughout the world who live and die
In poverty or hunger.
Give them, through our hands
this day their daily bread,
And by our understanding love,
Give peace and joy.

Mother Teresa, Calcutta

Burden Bearer

If any little help may ease
The burden of another,
God give me love and care and strength
To help along a brother.

Help me to build people up
Not tear them down.

Margaret Fishback Powers

Billy McBone

Billy McBone
Had a mind of his own,
Which he mostly kept under his hat.
The teachers all thought
That he couldn't be taught,
But Bill didn't seem to mind that.

Billy McBone
Had a mind of his own,
Which the teachers had searched for for years.
Trying test after test,
They still never guessed
It was hidden between his ears.

Billy McBone
Had a mind of his own,
Which only his friends ever saw.
When the teacher said, "Bill,
Whereabouts is Brazil?"
He just shuffled and stared at the floor.

Billy McBone
Had a mind of his own,
Which he kept under lock and key.
While the teachers in vain
Tried to burgle his brain,
Bill's thoughts were off wandering free.

Allan Ahlberg

On Ageing

When you see me sitting quietly,
Like a sack left on the shelf,
Don't think I need your chattering,
I'm listening to myself.
Hold! Stop! Don't pity me!
Hold! Stop your sympathy!
Understanding if you got it,
Otherwise I'll do without it!

When my bones are stiff and aching
And my feet won't climb the stairs,
I will only ask one favor:
Don't bring me no rocking chair.

When you see me walking, stumbling,
Don't study and get it wrong.
'Cause tired don't mean lazy
And every goodbye ain't gone.
I'm the same person I was back then,
A little less hair, a little less chin,
A lot less lungs and much less wind,
But ain't I lucky I can still breathe in.

Maya Angelou

Slavery

Got one mind for the boss to see,
Got another mind for what I know is me.

Anonymous – Afro-American

Dear Father

Dear Father, help me with the love
That casteth out all fear.
Teach me to lean on thee, and feel
That thou art very near;
That no temptation is unseen,
No childish grief too small,
Since thou, with patience infinite,
Dost soothe and comfort all.

Louisa M. Alcott

It's nice to be important
but it's more important to be nice.

Traditional

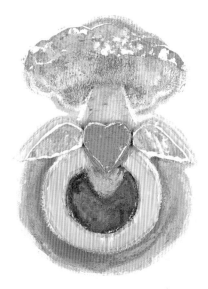

Little deeds of kindness,
Little words of love,
Help to make earth happy,
Like the heavens above.

Julia Carney

Benediction

Thanks to the ear
that someone may hear

Thanks to seeing
that someone may see

Thanks to feeling
that someone may feel

Thanks to the touch
that one may be touched

Thanks to the flowering of white moon
and spreading shawl of black night
holding villages and cities together

James Berry

68

Childhood

I used to think that grown-up people chose
To have stiff backs and wrinkles round their nose,
And veins like small fat snakes on either hand,
On purpose to be grand.
Till through the banisters I watched one day
My great-aunt Etty's friend who was going away,
And how her onyx beads had come unstrung.
I saw her grope to find them as they rolled;
And then I knew that she was helplessly old,
As I was helplessly young.

Frances Cornford

69

FUTURE PERFECT

Sit or lie with your spine straight, one hand resting lightly on your tummy, the other hand on your heart. Imagine breathing through your heart. Close your eyes and think about something that makes you feel wonderful; your favorite place; your favorite holiday; snuggling up in a warm, soft blanket; being hugged by someone special – whatever makes you feel happy.

Now feel that wonderful feeling begin to spread, out from your heart, through your chest and out through your body until you feel wonderful all over. Feel yourself expanding with that wonderful feeling. Imagine yourself begin to lift off the ground, rising higher and higher until you are floating and gliding way up in the sky and looking down upon the earth beneath you. As you look down you see the most beautiful rainbow you have ever seen! You float down to sit right on top of it . . . feel the vibrant colors of the rainbow almost becoming part of you. This is a magic rainbow and the world beneath you is the world of the future, the perfect future filled with love, the future as you would want it to be. Look down . . . what do you see in your perfect world? Notice the colors and the sounds. How are the people treating each other ? What are they talking about ? . . . Now, take some of all the love you have in your heart and send it down to all the people on earth . . . watch how good it makes them feel . . . feel the love come back to you, even stronger than it was when you sent it out . . . feel it fill you up! As the earth beneath you returns to our time, keep sending love from your heart to the people on the earth . . . the more love you send, the more you are filled with love.

As you prepare to leave your magic rainbow, know that the earth will always feel a little better because of the love you sent. Slowly now, glide away from the rainbow knowing you can return anytime you want. Gradually you return to earth, until you land gently back where you are right now. Feel your heartbeat now, your breathing, your body and the room around you. See if you can still feel that warm, wonderful feeling inside you and whenever you're ready, you can open your eyes.

Jennifer Day

SMALL
THINGS
THAT
HAVE
NO
WORDS

Small Things

Dear Father
hear and bless
Thy beasts and singing birds:
And guard
with tenderness
small things
that have no words.

Anonymous

Three Little Owls Who Sang Hymns

There were three little owls in a wood
Who sang hymns whenever they could;
What the words were about
One could never make out,
But one felt it was doing them good.

Anonymous

The Tickle Rhyme

"Who's that tickling my back?"
said the wall.
"Me," said a small
caterpillar. "I'm learning
to crawl."

Ian Serraillier

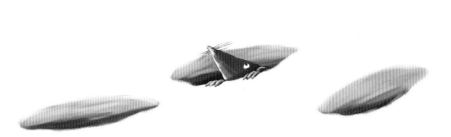

Small, Smaller

I thought that I knew all there was to know
Of being small, until I saw once, black against the snow,
A shrew, trapped in my footprint, jump and fall
And jump again and fall, the hole too deep, the walls too tall.

Russell Hoban

Cat Kisses

Sandpaper kisses
on a cheek or a chin –
that is the way
for a day to begin!

Sandpaper kisses –
a cuddle, a purr.
I have an alarm clock
that's covered with fur.

Bobbi Katz

The Donkey

I saw a donkey
One day old,
His head was too big
For his neck to hold;
His legs were shaky
And long and loose,
They rocked and staggered
And weren't much use.

He tried to gambol
And frisk a bit,
But he wasn't quite sure
Of the trick of it.
His queer little coat
Was soft and grey,
And curled at his neck
In a lovely way.

He looked so little
And weak and slim,
I prayed the world
Might be good to him.

Gertrude Hind

Something Told the Wild Geese

Something told the wild geese
  It was time to go.
Though the field lay golden
  Something whispered, "Snow."
Leaves were green and stirring,
  Berries, lustre-glossed,
But beneath warm feathers
  Something cautioned, "Frost."
All the sagging orchards
  Steamed with amber spice,
But each wild breast stiffened
  At remembered ice.
Something told the wild geese
  It was time to fly –
Summer sun was on their wings,
  Winter in their cry.

Rachel Field

Michael's Song

Because I have set no snare
  But leave them flying free,
All the birds of the air
  Belong to me.

From the blue-tit on the sloe
  To the eagle on the height,
Uncaged they come and go
  For my delight.

And so the sunward way
  I soar on the eagle's wings,
And in my heart all day
  The blue-tit sings.

Wilfrid Gibson

The Caged Bird

You can catch me, you can bind me,
You can tether me and tie me,
You can lock me in a cage of gold
And fasten tight my wings;
You can treat me as your property,
Release me three times daily,
But you cannot trap my spirit
And you cannot steal my song.

Veronica Bennetts

Goldfish

The scene of the crime
was a goldfish bowl
goldfish were kept
in the bowl at the time:

that was the scene
and that was the crime

Alan Jackson

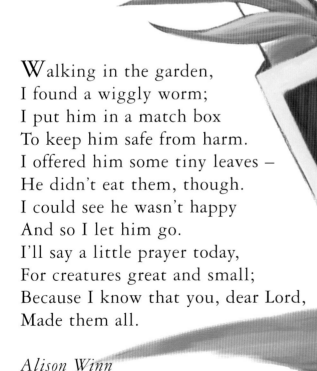

Walking in the garden,
I found a wiggly worm;
I put him in a match box
To keep him safe from harm.
I offered him some tiny leaves –
He didn't eat them, though.
I could see he wasn't happy
And so I let him go.
I'll say a little prayer today,
For creatures great and small;
Because I know that you, dear Lord,
Made them all.

Alison Winn

Wasp Poem

Today I drowned a wasp that I
Found floating in my wine.
Its life no longer is its own,
but neither is it mine.
With cool precision turned by hate
I drowned it in the sink –
it struggled in the water
but I didn't stop to think.
I didn't feel a pang at all,
I didn't change my mind,
I didn't even, really feel
that this was cruel, unkind.
If metamorphosis exists
perhaps a wasp I'll be
and won't feel resentment
if you do the same to me.
I may regret the sunshine,
the pollen and the jam,
but I'll understand you're drowning me
because I'm what I am.

Verity Bargate

I saw a Jolly Hunter

I saw a jolly hunter
  With a jolly gun
Walking in the country
  In the jolly sun.

    In the jolly meadow
      Sat a jolly hare
    Saw the jolly hunter,
      Took jolly care.

        Hunter jolly eager –
          Sight of jolly prey.
        Forgot gun pointing
          Wrong jolly way.

        Jolly hunter jolly head
          Over heels gone.
        Jolly old safety catch
          Not jolly on.

          Bang went the jolly gun.
            Hunter jolly dead.
          Jolly hare got clean away.
            Jolly good, I said.

Charles Causley

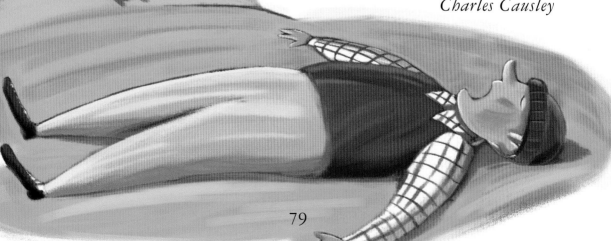

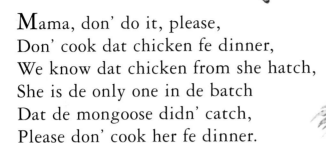

Chicken Dinner

Mama, don' do it, please,
Don' cook dat chicken fe dinner,
We know dat chicken from she hatch,
She is de only one in de batch
Dat de mongoose didn' catch,
Please don' cook her fe dinner.

Mama, don' do it, please,
Don' cook dat chicken fe dinner,
Yuh mean to tell mi yuh feget
Yuh promise her to we as a pet
She not even have a chance to lay yet
An yuh want to cook her fe dinner.

Mama, don' do it, please,
Don' cook dat chicken fe dinner,
Don' give Henrietta de chop,
Ah tell yuh what, we could swop,
We will get yuh one from de shop,
If yuh promise not to cook her fe dinner.

Mama, me really glad, yuh know,
Yuh never cook Henny fe dinner,
An she glad too, ah bet,
Oh Lawd, me suddenly feel upset,
Yuh don' suppose is somebody else pet
We eating now fe dinner?

Valerie Bloom

When All the World's Asleep

Where do insects go at night,
When all the world's asleep?
Where do bugs and butterflies
And caterpillars creep?
Turtles sleep inside their shells;
The robin has her nest.
Rabbits and the sly old fox
Have holes where they can rest.
Bears can crawl inside a cave;
The lion has his den.
Cows can sleep inside the barn,
And pigs can use their pen.
But where do bugs and butterflies
And caterpillars creep,
When everything is dark outside
And all the world's asleep?

Anita E. Posey

He Prayeth Best

He prayeth best who loveth best
All things both great and small,
For the dear God who loveth us
He made and loveth all.

Samuel Taylor Coleridge

81

TRANSFORMATION

Sit or lie with your spine straight, in a relaxed position. Place one hand on your heart and the other on your tummy. Close your eyes and listen to your breathing. Now feel your heartbeat . . . think of something that makes you feel happy; cuddling your favorite pet, swimming with dolphins in the warm, blue ocean, – whatever makes you feel wonderful . . . Now hold that wonderful feeling in your heart and just relax . . . Now imagine yourself sitting or lying under your favorite tree. Right next to you is a small pile of leaves. Reach out and feel the moist texture of the leaves and enjoy the feeling of peace and safety around you.

Now, imagine yourself becoming smaller, smaller and smaller, until you are so small that you can fit underneath one of the leaves. Think of yourself becoming a caterpillar crawling around under the leaf and then on top of it. Bite into the leaf and taste what it's like as you chew and swallow it. Notice how it feels . . . and as you eat, you begin to grow. You grow until you have outgrown your skin and you begin to shed it. You crawl over to a tiny branch on the tree and you spin threads of silk onto a twig and then button it all around you until you are hanging from the twig inside the button of silk. As you hang there, nice and relaxed, you feel yourself begin to transform again as you become covered in a golden chrysalis shell. It is very safe and peaceful.

Your chrysalis begins to open and slowly you discover that you have wings . . . and beautiful colors . . . magically you have become a butterfly! How does it feel to be you now? Gradually your wings unfold and lift you up into the air. You find yourself flying, up between the branches of your tree, darting from leaf to leaf, fluttering in and out of the warm sunbeams. Now landing softly on the pile of leaves you rest and relax . . . and slowly, gradually, you transform back into yourself. Take a deep breath and see if you feel that wonderful feeling inside you. Can you make it spread all the way through your body, until you feel like one big smile? Now whenever you're ready, you can open your eyes.

Jennifer Day

THE

MOON

SEES ME

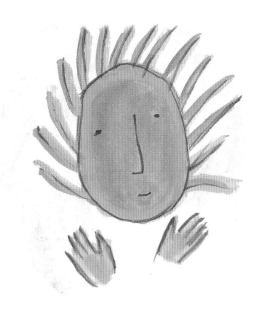

from *A Morning Song –*
For the First Day of Spring

Morning has broken
Like the first morning,
Blackbird has spoken
  Like the first bird.
Praise for the singing!
Praise for the morning!
Praise for them, springing
  Fresh from the Word!

Eleanor Farjeon

The earth does not belong to man; man belongs to the earth.

Chief Seattle

Sun Is Laughing

This morning she got up
on the happy side of bed,
pulled back
the grey sky-curtains
and she poked her head
through the blue window
of heaven,
her yellow laughter
spilling over,
falling broad across the grass,
brightening the washing on the line,
giving more shine
to the back of a ladybug
and buttering up all the world.

Then, without any warning,
as if she was suddenly bored,
or just got sulky
because she could hear no one
giving praise
to her shining ways,
Sun slammed the sky-window close,
plunging the whole world
into greyness once more.
O sun, moody one,
how can we live
without the holiday of your face?

Grace Nichols

Little Raindrops

Oh, where do you come from
  You little drops of rain,
Pitter patter, pitter patter,
  Down the window pane?

They won't let me walk,
  And they won't let me play,
And they won't let me go
  Out of doors at all today.

They put away my playthings
  Because I broke them all,
And then they locked up all my bricks,
  And they took away my ball.

Tell me, little raindrops,
  Is that the way you play,
Pitter patter, pitter patter,
  All the rainy day?

They say I'm very naughty
  But I've nothing else to do
But sit here at the window;
  I should like to play with you.

The little raindrops cannot speak,
  "But pitter patter pat,"
Means, "We can play on *this* side,
  Why can't we play on *that*?"

Jane Euphemia Browne

86

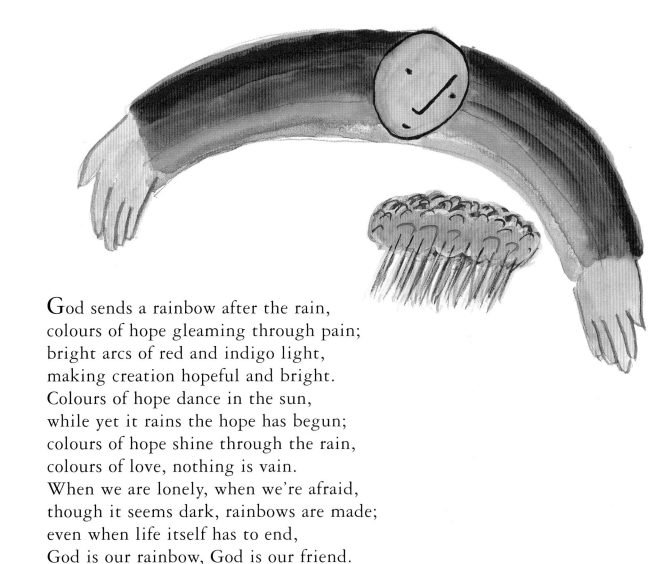

God sends a rainbow after the rain,
colours of hope gleaming through pain;
bright arcs of red and indigo light,
making creation hopeful and bright.
Colours of hope dance in the sun,
while yet it rains the hope has begun;
colours of hope shine through the rain,
colours of love, nothing is vain.
When we are lonely, when we're afraid,
though it seems dark, rainbows are made;
even when life itself has to end,
God is our rainbow, God is our friend.

Michael Forster

Praise

Praise the Lord for all the seasons,
　Praise Him for the gentle spring,
Praise the Lord for glorious summer,
　Birds and beasts and everything.
Praise the Lord who sends the harvest,
　Praise Him for the winter snows;
Praise the Lord, all ye who love Him,
　Praise Him, for all things He knows.

Mary Anderson

Kite

A kite on the ground
is just paper and string
but up in the air
it will dance and sing.
A kite in the air
will dance and will caper
but back on the ground
is just string and paper.

Anonymous

Four Seasons

Spring is showery, flowery, bowery.
Summer: hoppy, choppy, poppy.
Autumn: wheezy, sneezy, freezy.
Winter: slippy, drippy, nippy.

Anonymous

Comet

The night crackles with silence
As you fly
Headlong among the stars
Against dark granite
You are a spray of hot gold
Fiery plume of an ancient creature
Frivolous stroke of a molten pen
Breathless orange curve
You cut through boundless sky
A fiery race to the future
A dazzle of a second
A moment of the past

Zaro Weil

Praisèd be my Lord

Praisèd be my Lord God for all his creatures,
and especially our brother the sun,
who brings us the day and brings us the light;
fair is he and shines with a great splendour;
O Lord, he signifies to us thee.

Praisèd be my Lord for our sister the moon,
and for the stars, which he has set clear
and lovely in the heaven.

Praisèd be my Lord for our brother the wind,
and for air and cloud, calms and all weather,
by which thou upholdest life in all creatures.

Praisèd be my Lord for our sister water,
who is very serviceable unto us
and humble and precious and clean.

Praisèd be my Lord for our brother fire,
through whom thou givest light in the darkness;
and he is bright and pleasant and very mighty and strong.

Praisèd be my Lord for our mother the earth,
who doth sustain and keep us,
and bringest forth divers fruits
and flowers of many colours, and grass.

Praise ye and bless ye the Lord,
and give thanks unto him,
and serve him with great humility.
Amen

St. Francis of Assisi

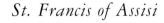

91

Flying

I saw the moon,
One windy night,
Flying so fast –
All silvery white –
Over the sky
Like a toy balloon
Loose from its string –
A runaway moon.
The frosty stars
Went racing past,
Chasing her on
Ever so fast.
Then everyone said,
"It's the clouds that fly,
And the stars and the moon
Stand still in the sky."
But I don't mind –
I saw the moon
Sailing away
Like a toy
Balloon.

J. M. Westrup

from *The Star*

Twinkle, twinkle, little star,
How I wonder what you are!
Up above the world so high,
Like a diamond in the sky.

When the blazing sun is gone,
When he nothing shines upon,
Then you show your little light,
Twinkle, twinkle all the night.

Jane Taylor

I Never See the Stars at Night

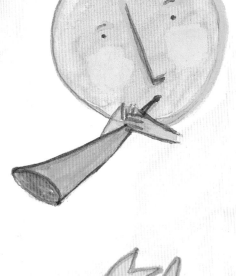

I never see the stars at night
    waltzing round the Moon
without wondering why they dance when
    no one plays a tune.

I hear no fiddles in the air
    or high and heavenly band
but round about they dance, the stars
    for ever hand in hand.

I think that wise ventriloquist
    the Old Man in the Moon
whistles so that only stars
    can hear his magic tune.

George Barker

Hurricane

Shut the windows
Bolt the doors
Big rain coming
Climbing up the mountain

Neighbors whisper
Dark clouds gather
Big rain coming
Climbing up the mountain

Gather in the clotheslines
Pull down the blinds
Big wind rising
Coming up the mountain

Branches falling
Raindrops flying
Treetops swaying
People running
Big wind blowing
Hurricane! on the mountain.

Dionne Brand

When the Sun Rises

When the sun rises, I go to work,
When the sun goes down, I take my rest,
I dig the well from which I drink,
I farm the soil that yields my food,
I share creation, Kings can do no more.

Anonymous, Chinese (2500 BC)

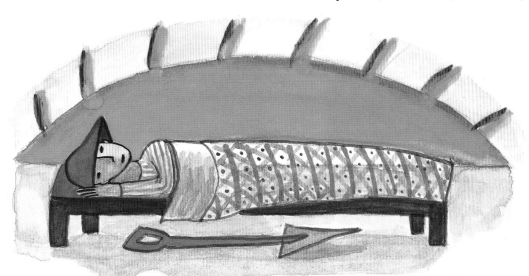

I See the Moon

I see the moon,
And the moon sees me;
God bless the moon,
And God bless me.

Anonymous

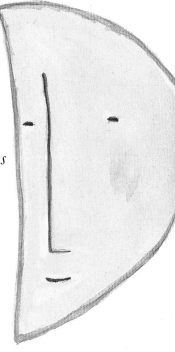

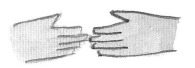

A RAINBOW MEDITATION

God sends a rainbow after the rain . . .
Colors of hope gleaming through pain . . .

Do you love to see rainbows lighting up the sky ?
Can you see a rainbow in your imagination now ?

Sit down quietly somewhere and close your eyes.
Use your 'inner eyes' to imagine a bright six-pointed
star shining over the whole world.

Can you see how every ray of light becomes a beautiful
rainbow reaching down to every country ?

Imagine the rainbows are taking healing to people who are unhappy or sick
today, and taking peace to countries where there is war.

Each of the colors of the rainbow contains a special gift
from the magical angels of the healing star:

RED imagine a soft pink red bringing the gift of LOVE.
ORANGE this color brings the gift of COURAGE
to stand up for what is good and true.
YELLOW this bright shining golden color of the sun brings the gift of
HAPPINESS. It helps everyone feel hopeful and to think happy thoughts.
GREEN this is the color of nature and so many beautiful things on our Mother
Earth. Green brings the gift of HEALING to our planet. Imagine this lovely
green light bringing a good harvest (so everyone has enough to eat), happy
healthy rain forests, and well being for all animals, birds and the world
of nature.
BLUE imagine a gentle blue light (almost like moonlight) shining into all the
rivers, seas and oceans of our planet to clean away all pollution. Picture all the
sea creatures, the fishes, whales and dolphins swimming happily in their clean
water. "Thank you for our gift," they say.
INDIGO this darker blue light brings the gifts of PEACE and COMFORT.
It's like a lovely blue cloak. If you know anyone who is not well today,
see this light wrapped around them, soothing away all their pain.
VIOLET this color helps us turn our thoughts towards God. Thank you God
for all the beauties of our planet. Thank you trees and flowers, for animals and
birds. Thank you God for the Sun, the Moon, the Stars . . .
and . . . for rainbows.

Jenny Dent

THE
SEAS
ARE MY
GREEN
ROBE

Only when the last tree has died
and the last river has been poisoned
and the last fish has been caught
will we realize that we cannot eat money.

19th-Century Cree Indian

Spell of the Earth

I am the round of the globe,
The seas are my green robe,
I am where all plants grow
    And the trees know

From me they draw their strength,
From me all stems find length.
I am rich in countless ways,
    All footsteps give me praise.

Elizabeth Jennings

from *All Things Bright and Beautiful*

All things bright and beautiful,
All creatures great and small,
All things wise and wonderful,
The Lord God made them all.

Each little flower that opens,
Each little bird that sings,
He made their glowing colours,
He made their tiny wings.

He gave us eyes to see them,
And lips that we might tell,
How great is God Almighty,
Who has made all things well.

Cecil Frances Alexander

If you have plenty, be not greedy,
But share it with the poor and needy:
If you have a little, take good care
To give the little birds a share.

Traditional

Countdown

*H*urry, cried Progress,
and on to Earth
rushed

chain saw, axe and JCB,
Crop sprays, oil slicks, pesticide;
battery farms and DDT,
smog and tear gas, monoxide.
Additives and sonic boom,
pills and parking lots,
concrete jungles, filled with gloom,
high-rise concrete flats.
Nuclear waste for just a taste
of what is still to come;
settle down, our shelter's warm –
do make yourself at home!
We've cigarettes to blacken lungs –
who needs seeds and forestry
with acid rain to kill?

Come in, come in! cried Progress.
Let's light these cloudy skies –
and crept towards the button,
rubbing smoke-filled eyes.

Welcome, daughters,
to your land –
this ark is yours and mine.
Do watch your step,
the trap is set –
we only wait for Time.

Come in, my sons,
do feel at home;
come in and share the mirth!
I've played my part –
you alone
can rescue planet Earth.

Judith Nichol

Moment

Among the dustbins
and scrawny cats
yellowing newspapers
and broken slats
a moment of beauty
breaks in the gutter
as rainclouds part
and the moon peeps
and is caught
in a rainbow puddle
of oil-slicked water.

Cecil Rajendra

Four Little Tigers

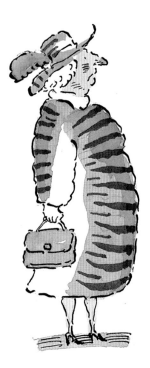

Four little tigers
Sitting in a tree;
One became a lady's coat –
And now there are three.

Three little tigers
'Neath a sky of blue;
One became a rich man's rug –
Now there's only two.

Two little tigers
Sitting in the sun;
One a hunter's trophy made –
Now there's only one.

One little tiger
Waiting to be had;
Oops! He got the hunter first –
Aren't you kind of glad?

Frank Jacobs

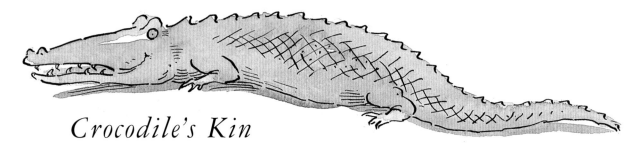

Crocodile's Kin

The best use for a crocodile skin
Is to keep a crocodile's insides in.

Colin McNaughton

The Rose, The Weed and Lucy

The rose to the weed
Said "God had no need
To create things like you
Who have nothing to do
Except spoil
Nice clean soil."

The rose to the weed
Said "You and your breed
Are just pests on this earth
With no beauty or worth.
We grow tall
While you sprawl."

The rose to the weed
Said "Ladies take heed
Of the way that we grow
Saying – Oh, what a show! –
But at you
They pooh-pooh".

Now later that day
Lucy ran out to play
And was led by her nose
To the beautiful rose –
Its bright petals
And sepals,

And "Oh, you sweet bloom,
Come and perfume my room
With your scent," Lucy said
As she cut off its head –
Naughty child –
The weed smiled.

Richard Edwards

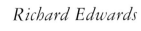

How Can One Sell the Air?

We shall consider your offer
to buy our land.
What is it that the White Man wants to buy?
my people will ask.

How can one sell the air
or buy the warmth of the earth?
It is difficult for us to imagine.
If we don't own the sweet air
or the bubbling water,
how can you buy it from us?
Each hillside of pines shining in the sun,
each sandy beach and rocky river bank,
every steep valley with bees humming
or mists hanging in dark woods,
has been made sacred by some event
in the memory of our people.

We are part of the earth
and the earth is part of us.
The fragrant flowers are our sisters;
the reindeer, the horse,
the great eagles, are our brothers.
The foamy crests of waves in the river,
the sap of meadow flowers,
the pony's sweat and the man's sweat
are one and the same thing.
So when the Great Chief in Washington
sends word that he wants to buy all these things,
we find it hard to understand.

Chief Seattle

Rainforest

The forest drips and glows with green.
The tree-frog croaks his far-off song.
His voice is stillness, moss and rain
drunk from the forest ages long.

We cannot understand that call
unless we move into his dream,
where all is one and one is all
and frog and python are the same.

We with our quick dividing eyes
measure, distinguish and are gone.
The forest burns, the tree-frog dies,
yet one is all and all are one.

Judith Wright

105

The Seed

How does it know,
this little seed,
if it is to grow
to a flower or weed,
if it is to be
a vine or a shoot,
or grow to a tree
with a long deep root?
A seed so small
where do you suppose
it stores up all
of the things it knows?

Aileen Fisher

For flowers that bloom about our feet,
Father we thank thee.
For tender grass so fresh, so sweet,
Father we thank thee.
For the song of bird and hum of bee,
For all things fair we hear or see,
Father in heaven, we thank thee.

Ralph Waldo Emerson

Goodnight! Goodnight!
Far flies the light;
But still God's love
Shall flame above
Making all bright.
Goodnight! Goodnight!

Victor Hugo

A WALK IN THE COUNTRY

Come on – we're going to run down the country lane together – right now! How? It's easy – lie down and make yourself as comfortable as you possibly can. Gently close your eyes. Take a deep breath in, breathing through your nose. As you breathe in slowly push your tummy out as far as you can and then as you breathe out through your nose, let your tummy fall gently. Take another deep breath in and imagine that you are breathing in all the calmness in the world. As you breathe out, feel yourself becoming very relaxed – maybe there are places in your body where it feels as if coiled springs are unwinding. Take another deep breath in and out and feel that your eyelids are becoming heavier and heavier – you can open them anytime you want to, but you don't want to. Now reach out and hold my hand and we can skip along our own country lane.

It's Spring and the trees are very green. Can you hear the birds? It's just been raining and there are puddles – let's jump in them – never mind if our socks get wet. Can you smell the fresh country air? Mmmm I can smell cut grass, wild flowers and the moist earth from the rain – what about you? We're coming to the end of our lane now; there's a gate at the end. Let's climb over it and race across that field. You're faster than me! I'm going to sit down in the grass by the stream – can you hear the water rushing past? The sun's out now and I'm watching the rays make the stream all glittery. I'm lying down looking up at the blue sky – you're lying next to me and I can see the sun on your hair.
We've had a lovely time.

Take another deep breath in slowly and as you breathe out
you can open your eyes whenever you feel ready.
See you next time in the lane.

Amanda Slade

THERE

IS A

TIME

And so my fellow Americans, ask not what your country can do for you; ask what you can do for your country.

My fellow citizens of the world, ask not what America will do for you, but what together we can do for the freedom of man.

John F. Kennedy 1961

Lord of the Morning

Lord of the morning
and ruler of all seasons,
hear our prayer
and have mercy on our souls.
Shine upon me, Lord
and I shall be light like the day.

Syrian Orthodox

from *Imagine*

Imagine there's no heaven
It's easy if you try.
No hell below us,
Above us only sky.
Imagine all the people,
Living for today.

Imagine there's no countries
It isn't hard to do,
Nothing to kill or die for
And no religion too.
Imagine all the people
Living life in peace.
You may say I'm a dreamer,
But I'm not the only one.
I hope some day you'll join us
And the world will be as one.

John Lennon

Out of the experience of an extraordinary human disaster that lasted too long must be born a society of which all humanity will be proud . . . Each time one of us touches the soil of this land, we feel a sense of personal renewal. The national mood changes as the seasons change. We are moved by a sense of joy and exhilaration when the grass turns green and the flowers bloom . . . We pledge ourselves to liberate all our people from the continuing bondage of poverty, deprivation, suffering, gender and other discrimination . . . Let freedom reign. The sun shall never set on so glorious a human achievement. God bless Africa.

Nelson Mandela

The Serenity Prayer

God grant me
the serenity to
accept the things
I cannot change,
courage to change
the things I can,
and wisdom
to know the
difference.

Anonymous

I would be true, for there are those who trust me,
  I would be pure, for there are those who care,
I would be strong, for there is much to suffer,
  I would be brave, for there is much to dare,
I would be a friend of all, the foe, the friendless,
  I would be giving and forget the gift,
I would be humble, for I know my weakness,
  I would look up, and laugh and love and live.

Anonymous

New Leaf

Today is the first day of my new book.
I've written the date
and underlined it
in red felt-tip
with a ruler.
I'm going to be different
with this book.

With this book
I'm going to be good.
With this book
I'm always going to do the date like
that
dead neat
with a ruler
just like Christine Robinson.

With this book
I'll be as clever as Graham Holden,
get all my sums right, be as
neat as Mark Veitch;
I'll keep my pens and pencils
in a pencil case
and never have to borrow again.

With this book
I'm going to work hard,
not talk, be different —
with this book,
not yell out, mess about,
be silly —
with this book.

with this book
I'll be grown-up, sensible,
and every one will want me;
I'll be picked out first
like Iain Cartwright:
no one will ever laugh at me again.
Everything will be
different

with this book . . .

Mick Gower

Happy Thought

The world is so full
of a number of things,
I'm sure we should all
be as happy as kings.

Robert Louis Stevenson

There Isn't Time!

There isn't time, there isn't time
To do the things I want to do,
With all the mountain-tops to climb,
And all the woods to wander through,
And all the seas to sail upon,
And everywhere there is to go,
And all the people, every one
Who lives upon the earth to know.
There's only time, there's only time
To know a few, and do a few,
And then sit down and make a rhyme
About the rest I want to do.

Eleanor Farjeon

116

Leisure

What is this life if, full of care,
We have no time to stand and stare.

No time to stand beneath the boughs
And stare as long as sheep or cows.

No time to see, when woods we pass,
Where squirrels hide their nuts in grass.

No time to see, in broad daylight,
Streams full of stars like stars at night.

No time to turn at Beauty's glance,
And watch her feet, how they can dance.

No time to wait till her mouth can
Enrich that smile her eyes began.

A poor life this if, full of care,
We have no time to stand and stare.

William Henry Davies

Drop thy still dews of quietness,
till all our strivings cease;
take from our souls the strain and stress,
and let our ordered lives confess
the beauty of thy peace.

John Greenleaf Whittier

Each time a man stands up for an ideal,
or acts to improve the lot of others,
or strikes out against injustice,
he sends forth a tiny ripple of hope
and crossing each other from a million
different centers of energy and daring,
those ripples build a current that can
sweep down the mightiest walls
of oppression and resistance.

Robert Kennedy 1966

There is a time for everything,
and a season for every activity under heaven:
a time to be born and a time to die,
a time to plant and a time to uproot,
a time to kill and a time to heal,
a time to tear down and a time to build,
a time to weep and a time to laugh,
a time to mourn and a time to dance,
a time to scatter stones and a time to gather them,
a time to embrace and a time to refrain,
a time to search and a time to give up,
a time to keep and a time to throw away,
a time to tear and a time to mend,
a time to be silent and a time to speak,
a time to love and a time to hate,
a time for war and a time for peace.

Ecclesiastes 3, v 1-8

THERE IS A TIME

Lie or sit down keeping the body open and relaxed. Close your eyes and gently listen keeping your attention completely on what you are hearing.

A friend of mine has a favorite saying about time: "If you live in the past, you stay there. If you live in the future, it never arrives.
The only time to live is in the present, now."

That probably sounds like a bit of a riddle. But then if you stop and think about it, time is something of a puzzle anyway. When you're bored, it drags its feet so that minutes seem to stretch into hours. And yet when you're having fun, it flies by so fast that hours shrink into minutes. Why does it do that?

Well, time doesn't really shrink or stretch at all. It's all in our minds. Whenever we're really interested in what we're doing or are simply having a fun time, we're so involved in what we are doing that we don't notice the time passing. We probably don't even notice ourselves thinking either. That's because all our energy is going into what we are doing. So much so that there is no energy left over to feed unnecessary thoughts. On the other hand, when we're not really involved in what we're doing there is nowhere for our energy to go but into our thoughts. Instead of us using our minds to channel our energy and thoughts into whatever we are doing, our minds – or rather, our thoughts – use us. And because our thoughts travel faster than the speed of light we can think an awful lot of thoughts in a very short space of time. So many thoughts, in fact, that we end up under the illusion that more time has passed than really has. The illusion is even stronger because these thoughts tend to be all over the place. They're off in the past or in the future.

They're in front of the TV or at our friends' houses.
In fact, they're absolutely everywhere except where we are now.
That's why a lot of people learn to meditate. Some people describe meditation as a way of learning to master their thoughts rather than have their thoughts master them. But really meditation is simply learning to be fully present, in the here and now, in such a way that unnecessary thoughts don't even arise. More than that, when you've learned to be totally here, right now, you will not only be living in the present. You will also have mastered the secret of time.

Try it for yourself. But be patient. It can take a while to learn to live totally in the present. Yet once you've learned how to do it, the knack will stay with you for the rest of your life. Furthermore, you'll have all the time in the world. Because when you learn to live in the present you discover that now is eternal.

John Baldock

INDEX OF FIRST LINES

INDEX OF TITLES

INDEX OF AUTHORS

ACKNOWLEDGEMENTS

For permission to reproduce copyright material in this book, the author and publishers gratefully acknowledge the following:

David Adam: Father, bless me to the dawn, from TIDES AND SEASONS (Triangle Books, 1989), by permission of SPCK, London; Allan Ahlberg: Billy McBone, from HEARD IT IN THE PLAYGROUND (Viking, 1989), copyright © Allan Ahlberg, 1989, reprinted by permission of Penguin Books Ltd; Dorothy Aldis: Bursting, from ALL TOGETHER, copyright 1952 by Dorothy Aldis, copyright renewed © 1980 by Roy E.Porter, reprinted by permission of G.P.Putnam's Sons; Maya Angelou: On Ageing, from AND STILL I RISE, copyright (c) 1978 by Maya Angelou, reprinted by permission of Random House Inc. Anonymous: Coloured, from the magazine of the King Edward VI Handsworth School, Birmingham, reprinted by permission of the school. I asked the Little Boy Who Cannot See, from SING PRAISES (Religious Education Press); Verity Bargate: Wasp Poem, from STRICTLY PRIVATE, edited by Roger McGough (Penguin Books), copyright © Verity Bargate, reproduced by permission of The Agency (London) Ltd. All rights reserved and enquiries to The Agency (London) Ltd, 24 Pottery Lane, London W11 4LZ fax: 0171 727 9037; George Barker: I Never See the Stars at Night and The House I go to in my Dreams, from AYLSHAM FAIR (Faber & Faber Ltd); Veronica Bennetts: The Caged Bird, from CASTING A SPELL AND OTHER POEMS, compiled by Angela Huth (Orchard Books); James Berry: Benediction, from CHAIN OF DAYS (Oxford University Press), reprinted by permission of the author Evelyn Beyer; Jump or Jiggle, from ANOTHER HERE AND NOW STORY BOOK by Lucy Sprague Mitchell (Dutton, 1937), copyright 1937 by E.P.Dutton, renewed © 1965 by Lucy Sprague Mitchell. Used by permission of Dutton Children's Books, a division of Penguin Books USA Inc; Valerie Bloom: Chicken Dinner, from DUPPY JAMBOREE (Cambridge University Press, 1992), reprinted by permission of the author and publisher; Dionne Brand: Hurricane, from A CARIBBEAN DOZEN by John Agard and Grace Nichols (Walker Books); Catullus: I Hate and I Love, (Poem no 85) from THE POEMS OF CATULLUS, translated by Peter Whigham (Penguin Classics, 1966), translation copyright © Penguin Books Limited, 1966, reprinted by permission of the publisher; Charles Causley: I Saw a Jolly Hunter, from FIGGIE HOBBIN (Macmillan) and I am the Song, from EARLY IN THE MORNING (Viking), reproduced by permission of David Higham Associates Ltd; Marchette Chute: Reading, from RHYMES ABOUT US (E.P.Dutton, 1974), copyright 1974 by Marchette Chute, reprinted by permission of Elizabeth Roach; Wendy Cope: An Attempt At Unrhymed Verse, from ANOTHER DAY ON YOUR FOOT AND I WOULD HAVE DIED by John Agard, Wendy Cope, et.al. (Faber & Faber Ltd), copyright © Wendy Cope, 1995; Frances Cornford: Childhood, from COLLECTED POEMS (1954), by permission of Dr Hugh Cornford; John Cunliffe: A Poem in My Pocket, from DARE YOU GO?, copyright © 1992 John Cunliffe, first published by Scholastic Ltd, reprinted by permission of the publisher; W.H.Davies: Leisure, from THE COMPLETE POEMS OF W.H.DAVIES (Jonathan Cape Ltd, 1940) by permission of the Executors of the W.H. Davies Estate and Random House UK Ltd; Berlie Doherty: Kieran, from WALKING ON AIR (Harper Collins/Lion Books), copyright © 1993 by Berlie Doherty, by permission of David Higham Associates Ltd; Bob Dylan: from Gotta Serve Somebody, from LYRICS 1962-1985 (Jonathan Cape Ltd, 1985), copyright © 1979, Special Rider Music. All rights reserved. International copyright secured. Reprinted by permission of Special Rider Music; Ecclesiastes 3, v 1-8: from THE AUTHORIZED VERSION OF THE BIBLE (The King James Bible), the rights in which are vested in the Crown, reproduced by permission of the Crown's Patentee, Cambridge University Press; Richard Edwards: The Word Party, from THE WORD PARTY (Lutterworth Press, 1986), reprinted by permission of the publisher and John Johnson (Authors' Agent) Ltd. The Rose, The Weed and Lucy and On the Move, from A MOUSE IN MY ROOF (Orchard Books, 1988), reprinted by permission of the author; Eleanor Farjeon: Waking Up, Good Morning, and There Isn't Time, from SILVER SAND AND SNOW (Michael Joseph Ltd), and A Morning Song, from THE CHILDRENS BELLS (Oxford University Press), reprinted by permission of David Higham Associates Ltd; Max Fatchen: Look Out!, from SONGS FOR MY DOG AND OTHER PEOPLE (Kestrel Books, 1980), copyright © Max Fatchen, 1980, reprinted by permission of Penguin Books Ltd and John Johnson (Authors' Agent) Ltd; Rachel Field: Something Told the Wild Geese, from POEMS, copyright 1934 Macmillan Publishing Company, copyright renewed © 1962 Arthur S.Pederson, reprinted by permission of Simon & Schuster Books for Young Readers, an imprint of Simon & Schuster Children's Publishing Division; Aileen Fisher: My Puppy and The Seed, from UP THE WINDY HILL (Abelard Schuman) and At Night, from OUT IN THE DARK AND DAYLIGHT POEMS (Harper Collins Inc), reprinted by kind permission of the author; Michael Forster: God sends a rainbow after the rain, copyright © Kevin Mayhew Ltd, Rattlesden, Bury St.Edmunds, Suffolk IP30 OSZ. Used by permission from THE CHILDREN'S HYMN BOOK, Licence No. 798060; Rose Fyleman: Singing-Time, from THE FAIRY GREEN, copyright 1923 by George H.Doran, Co, used by permission of Bantam Doubleday Dell Publishing Group, Inc and The Society of Authors as the Literary Representative of the Estate of Rose Fyleman; Martin Gardner: The Giggles, from NEVER MAKE FUN OF A TURTLE, MY SON ;Wilfrid Gibson: Michael's Song, from COLLECTED POEMS 1905-1935 (Macmillan), reprinted by permission of the publisher; Mick Gowar: New Leaf, from THIRD TIME LUCKY (Viking Kestrel, 1988), copyright © Mick Gowar, 1988, reprinted by permission of Penguin Books Ltd; Emily Hearn: My Friend, from HOCKEY CARDS AND HOPSCOTCH, reprinted by permission of ITP Nelson Canada; Russell Hoban: Small, Smaller, from THE PEDALLING MAN (Heinemann), reprinted by permission of David Higham Associates Ltd; Mary Ann Hobermann: Brother, from HELLO AND GOODBYE (Little, Brown & Co, 1959); Brian Howard: If I were a